ORNAMENT
OF
HONOUR

T0382524

ORNAMENT
OF
HONOUR

E. H. R.
ALTOUNYAN

1937
CAMBRIDGE
AT THE UNIVERSITY PRESS

The English versions of the quotations from the Odyssey, opposite and on page 105, are taken from T. E. Shaw's translation, by permission of Mr Bruce Rogers and the Oxford University Press.

CAMBRIDGE
UNIVERSITY PRESS

University Printing House, Cambridge CB2 8BS, United Kingdom

Cambridge University Press is part of the University of Cambridge.

It furthers the University's mission by disseminating knowledge in the pursuit of education, learning and research at the highest international levels of excellence.

www.cambridge.org
Information on this title: www.cambridge.org/9781107505155

© Cambridge University Press 1937

First published 1937
First paperback edition 2015

A catalogue record for this publication is available from the British Library

ISBN 978-1-107-50515-5 Paperback

T. E. LAWRENCE

May 19, 1935

σῆμά τέ μοι χεῦαι πολιῆς ἐπὶ θινὶ θαλάσσης,
ἀνδρὸς δυστήνοιο, καὶ ἐσσομένοισι πυθέσθαι·
ταῦτά τέ μοι τελέσαι πῆξαί τ' ἐπὶ τύμβῳ ἐρετμόν,
τῷ καὶ ζωὸς ἔρεσσον ἐὼν μετ' ἐμοῖς ἑτάροισιν.

"And heap over the ashes a mound at the edge of the sea
where the surf breaks white, for a token telling of an
unhappy man to aftertime; and when the rites are
completed fix above my mound the oar that
in life I pulled among my fellows."

ODYSSEY, XI. 75–78.

PRELUDE

PRELUDE

I

You never saw that crooked moon
Behind Aleppo's citadel:
You never saw it shine again
In Dorsetshire.
For you had died a week ago
And I live on, a man disguised,
Thinking our thoughts and gaieties.

Come, curse me for this solemn dirge,
Haltingly fashioned, word on word,
Protesting "Nought is changed at all
In the Universe."
It is a lie! You know it now,
As you sleep rotting, once a man,
Disjointed from our pleasant plan
Of sweet converse.

You smile at last: let us not talk but see
Each other's faces through the emptiness of loss,
Knowing that all is dross,
Save spirit and the vision self-contained.

Your eyes are blue—
So I've been told—
Your hair of course
Is purest gold,
Pedunculated souls like me
Only regret they cannot see
When blue is black and gold is lead
And all of you is wholly dead.

Be not alarmed: though waters rise
From small deep springs up to my eyes,
And all my body gently rocks
Waiting to feel electric shocks
Olympian,
Small cunning channels drain those tears
And blown is the fuse Empyrean.

So be it then, O Crooked Moon,
Setting behind Aleppo hills,
I set out on my journey, not alone,
To find you in the flesh and common bone.

II

The world is spinning and the minds thereon
Cannot but catch the habit of this world,
Rotating round some love, some faith, some plan
Set firmly, proudly, lustfully, in the core

4

Of our enduring souls: so spin we on:
And royally rotation bears her crop
Of homeliness, of treasure, and of fame,
Till comforted and dazzled, yea, and dazed
We sing aloud in unison of sound
The praises of our round Earth and our day.
Rotundity protrudes her busy womb,
Fecundity bears all her sons away,
Away into the silence of the tomb
Sink one by one our gyroscopes of clay.

Upon this curious scene there came a man,
Courageous, not in daring destiny to set
Some limit to his capability,
But rather in the faith that each new soul
That stepped within this circle cursed by Time,
Had power to break the thickening rind of use
Which threatens round Creation, could it keep
The flame white-hot yet searing not a flower.
And accident divine, to faith and flame
Added the frosty twinkle of a star
To which our spinning globe seemed—what it is.

How small a thing is space where all is air,
How noisy are our certainties when truth
Wraps round us her still mantle, which despair
Ruffles in vain in her blind restlessness.

Above the din, snuffing that spaceless air,
Wrapped in his wisp of truth and twinkling still
He stood a moment, then slipped neatly in.

What was the prize he sought? The answer comes
Flashing through soul's dark night—"Integrity".
Crashing the word sounds, as a sword on shield.
It is a word new-minted to express
His soul and mind, his body wrapped in flame
Carried across our stage swift, noiselessly.

Could fame intoxicate that deep sane mind?
Could honours manacle a soul self-freed?
Could ease inflate that body so inured
To discipline of sand's austerity?
Who knows, who knew,—but he?
Before his eyes the King's highway did curve
Rounding in deadly noose his living course:
A nod, a smile, a step and he was free.

For Monument—Ah, yes—We'll look around—
An empty stage. Romance has nothing on
This week. The next? Perhaps. To-day
His writings pile up in the mind their mass.
Heroes obscure in life, in art have found
The glory which some frailty has denied:
Why should he steep in words, stripping himself?
Why enter battle bloodless, shadowy?

The human heart beats on when we are dead.
Words have no blood to carry on their lives,
But words win strength of steel by radiance
Of spirit forced through alphabetic chinks.
Words beckoned him: and presently men saw
Those *Pillars* and the dead heroic strand
Odysseus peers on from antiquity.

Such was the man who, splendidly designed
For some great-seeming work, resigned
All his own masonries, steadfast not to bind
His spirit but to spirit:
And, as he laughed the laughter of a god
Who sees man's littleness and his own included,
Bubbling with mirth, where others merely brooded,
Watching the pageant where no self intruded,
He rode on triumphs justly interluded
With the fierce purging of a man's despair.

III

Drunk with this load of loss,
Bowed down by nothingness,
Tottering let's dig a fosse
To bury us.
Deep it need hardly be,
Six foot by two by three,

Dug in humanity,
Should hold the pus.
Phew! What a nasty smell
Sorrow can raise. No spell,
Perfume of memory,
Philosophy,
Can staunch the ceaseless flow
Trickling now fast, now slow,
Of bitterness.
Raging through hollow tooth
Memories—forsooth.
What, shall we paw once more
Life lived? Let's rather snore
Humped on the Present floor
Inconsolate.
Pain cracks the glass of Thought,
Cuts deeply into nought,
Turns all we ever sought
Into a scream.
Hope tries to mop the floor,
Truth stops her with a roar,
Courage peeps round the door—
Slam it again.
Bodies of friends have been
Present, through clearly seen
Images wherein we preen

8

Our plumed desire.
Bodies alive not dead:
Death has not left a shred
Of all that sumptuous bed
Imagination.
Distance we bring to heel,
Absence is Fancy's meal,
Hearts, man, can only reel
In dead Creation.
Spirit's a mockery,
Mind's but a lechery,
Body's a witchery,
Body's not there.
Where is the lime that sticks
Spirit to mind like bricks?
What Body's playing tricks?
Answer who dare.
Wrath hiccoughs now her fill,
Pain streaks a thinning rill,
There's no more drink to spill,
Boy, fetch that flare.

Out in the air at last
Let us forget the past!
Swift, silent, deep and fast
Down drives despair.

IV

Love me a little while.
Yes, I've loved you.
How easy 'tis to say it now
That you
Will never see or feel or say a thing
That's true
For me who say and feel.

Love me a little while,
I like it best
When you do smile at me
Spirit-caressed
And I do look at you
Twin-blest.

Love me a little while
I've long to live.
Not in forgetfulness
Would I seek rest,
Nor in the memory
Of what's been best
In your companionship.
No, no, I'd only slip
Into your room again
When I'm sore pressed.

V

Heigh-o there—O he's gone.
Hallo—you're back again;
And on the dusty plain
Lies his trajectory.
Heigh-o, behold we swing
To the end of our mental string,
And circle the world with the whirr
Of thought's sharp scimitar.
Hallo, we're back once more
Sucking twin straws from the core,
Ambrosia's distillate.
With a leap he shoots like a star
Over the garden gate,
And presently comes from afar
With spice neatly packed in a jar,
Then swinging out over the world
We traverse pale History
Seen through the laughter-encurled
Eyes of his treachery,
To drop him in depths without sound,
Prolific, mole-like, profound
Of erudite industry.
Heigh-o for the mind that would hold
One particle now that he's cold.

With a swoop he is back from his lair,
With a pluck he unloosens our hair,
With a snort he has puffed out the flare
Of our idolatry.

God's Truth! In the void let us spill
Sentiment, anguish, and pill
Made of our fate.
Heigh-o, hallo, soon or late
Comes, as we flicker or burn,
Peace. And who would return?

As for beauty and joy on-the-wing—
Into the void let this small thing
Of ours fall echoing.

VI

Up to the peak on low gear
Down again frictionless
Horizontal without stop
Fleeting without a tear
Humming and motionless
But for the flickering poles,
What in the name of our souls
Can, shall, stop us?

Mind lightly taking control
Looks on the drifting landscape
Sees how it best can escape
Curving disaster, curb zeal
Of metallic smooth-running steel wheel
That nothing can break—
While the spirit tears on into space
And the mind marks the pace.
Up, up that extravagant chain
Down on the sober plain
Hurtling through realms of thought
Treading on solid, on nought,
What can stop us?

Answer comes quiet through hell,
Uninhabited of all our dead:—
"Nothing can break the spell,
But clay body in its clay bed."

VII

A moment comes when Power infinite
Wraps quiet coil on coil within the soul
Till the whole being quivers, resolute to wing
Or creep or rend or hew its golden road
Across all life, now mute, subservient.

Happy the man who sees in such an hour
What follows on that moment big with power.
Music has notes to catch
The tone and rhythm of her loveliness,
And Poetry, word-purged, those words can fill
With meanings from her own packed soul distilled;
And colourists have always hues to match
Our radiant emptiness.
But he whose empire spans humanity
Has for his measure notches in the soul,
Has for his guidance frail wires finely drawn,
But through the senses and his fortitude.
No beacon here amid those myriad lights,
No certain voice in that loud market-place
Communing with the spirit, now turned sprite,
Now speaking with the majesty of God;
Communing with the spirit shrunk in hell
Or swelling on the breast of ecstasy.
But ceaselessly, as wave on wave allows
No respite to the pebbles' suck and surge,
So restlessly the spirit's tide must move
To touch and leave again each tiny cove
Set in the shore of our carnality.
Often the mind must long in weariness
To build snug harbours round accomplishment
Where deep and still the waters mirror back

A sky that seems to hold the truth clean hewn
Out of our wild conglomerate of fact;
And sometimes reason points to leafiness
Wherewith to build, wherein to hide itself,
And tabernacle mind when mind is spent.
Happy that man; though terrible the urge
That washed unceasing his white temple's shore
Built upon vision that could hourly sift
The silting minutes' treasure drifting in.
And if despair swept down out of a heaven
That opened vast, unlit, magnificent,
Unto the eye inturned and seeing all,
Yet the whole being steadfast to the storm
Rising and falling round his loneliness,
Could strip, could cull in mental nakedness
Contemplative, some rare intricate flower
Ever ablowing in that close-leafed bower.
Thus step by step on his own pilgrimage
He passed this way by Chaucer's antique road:
And only once his sword's full flame unsheathed
To carve initials for posterity.

A moment comes when power infinite
Wraps each new soul deep in temerity:
We rise to thrust in forward jollity
And fall soul-stripped on some neglected stone.

Or maybe happiness has swamped the heart,
Or golden beauty falls a gilded bird.
O everlasting noose undoing power,
O error multiplied as sunset tower,
Who shall escape your dazzling dream of death?
Therefore a moment, ere this darkness close,
Against the sunset of our memories
I hold this darkened mirror to our eyes
To show the immobile lineaments of man.
O words new-minted in the spirit's fire,
O images that throng this setting sheet,
O gnawing rhythm, bred of our own desire
To etch in steel this bitter ecstasy!

A moment comes: tense on the dark the wave
Breaks in warm laughter seething round our feet.

VIII

Let us experiment with Time,
Seeking in bliss
To reach some pertinent sublime
Something we miss.

Let us encompass us with doom
And stricken there,

Play on the bugles of some Time
One lively air.

One year, one month, one day
An hour, minute, second
Pass reverently down the way
By solemn ages beckoned.
But hours and hours of play
Disturbing the procession
Persistently astray
Disgraceful in secession,
Carry us when we are fey
Right out of time and our day.

Stones look up into our eyes,
Speaking of day's sunlight
Note in their stony surprise
Eyes laughing straight into night,
Centuries back when a friend
Strolled with us, asked us to lend
Some thing.
Or perhaps strong on the wing
Hours flitting fly out, fly in,
Weaving across present space
Intricate patterns of lace,
Catching sweet friends in the thrall
Of fancying they're within call.

But even hours are powerless,
And years have long been dead
To help us when we're dowerless
Of future joys. Instead
The playful hours mock us
The days, the nights but rock us,
Intelligence doth lock us
In present misery.
But who can rob the second
Striking through time's distress,
Flashing from all we've reckoned
Light in our wilderness,
Of vision's holy hours
Eternal echoing
Leading to future bowers,
Leafy continuing
Of seeds of lovely flowers
Long past their blossoming.

Blow out O small toy bugles
From all that stricken camp,
Not reason's brow that glowers,
Not muffled thoughtful hours
Shall blind that brilliant lamp.

Let us experiment in Time,
Use foreign rhyme,

Asking the minute to unlash
The second's flash,
From time's enlaced serene
O'erpolished black routine.

IX

O citadel of Thought, how solid stand
Those bastions on the outposts of the dark.
How green the swards of your secure pleasance
Where fancy plays the truant from those wars
Waged ceaselessly upon the outer works
That front the hosts of Logic and Despair.

Day rises, and the circling sun doth mark
His shadows on your serried masonries
And on those names engraved near armèd lights
Clear in romance with learned heraldries,
On which the soul looks, smiles, and turns away
To man the ramparts 'gainst the new-come day.
How cool the air we breathe beside the fount
Set in the court-yard shaded from the sun,
Wherein, entranced by learning's symmetry,
We scan the polished blocks which other men
Have hewn and set in humble industry:
While ever in that midmost circled space
The waters rise, speaking of running life.

Who that is sane would leave this citadel
To foray lonely like a dog distraught?
Who would forsake those mental battlements
To worship his own spirit's sacraments,
Cursed by black loneliness and noon's despair?
Who but the mad? Yet lonely on his hill
And looking back, what did he see and fear?

The sun is setting; dark the court and still,
Save for the tinkle of its starveling rill;
And all the walls flame back, now day is done,
The jealous hues of yellowing desire
To keep in darkness what the light has won.

Cold citadel that splendid through the night
Keeps in your dungeons prisoners of spite,
Where are the freemen late upon your walls?

Yet, shall a wanderer through the sands of time,
Leaving no mark of ruin tangible,
Avail for ought but self, prevail
More than the minute of his transience?

Enduring Spirit built but to abide
In other spirits, only those deride
Who loaf and strut in daylit palaces,
Leaving to Night Night's explanation.

Enduring spirit, staring into night
While carried steadfast on our wavering day,
Why seek, why question your frail permanence
When all your turrets gleam eternally!

FUGUE

FUGUE

I

The sky no longer holds that crooked moon,
A full-orbed light outshines the enfeebled stars,
Peace of a sort now settles, but too soon
To presage the defeat of this dim Mars.
Still from the vapours of the torrid day
Steals a miasma through the clear spread night,
Enfolding in a shroud the spirit's play
Contemplative, serene in dead moonlight.
From birth to death there is no settlement
For all the wars of passionate desire,
Waged for some timeless live embodiment
To crown our forcèd passage through this mire.
O temporal life! Not Christ, not incarnation,
Can ever atone this life and this frustration.

II

Of Courage men have oftentimes discoursed,
Ruffling bright-eyed in anecdotal train:
Many have told how they have lightly coursed
Monsters of steel, or flown that mountain chain.
I listen to this common talk of peers
And proudly join in flighting valiant words

To carry on the sound of deeds well done;
Holding that none who fear beneath the sun
But hold in their own hearts the avenging swords
To slay the dragon of their own hearts' fears.
I listen, and I miss from Chivalry
The ribald heart, the swift enlightening ply
Of mind in mind inturned; the outflung gay
Mockery of Self, holding its very soul at bay.

III

I know not whether reason at the last
Shall link the body to celestial fire,
Or spirit only must outlive the blast
And hurtle through the void and seek in ire
The God who thought it well to blind our eyes
To any meaning in His splendid skies.
I know not when our Reason at the last
Shall twitch away this swaddling holiness.
But this I know: His own obedient mind
Our spirit bears in imbecility
Shall forge at last the white-hot link designed
To join our chain to His infinity.
Meanwhile, if all have died in ignorance
Let His own mind beat out its impotence.

IV

Stars have no words to interfuse their spheres
Nor sun to vary his unbending ray;
When all Creation weeps she has but tears
To veil in rain the sorrows of her day.
A myriad facets can the mind oppose,
Articulate emblazoned heraldry,
To other minds set in these lists that close
Only with Night's uncouth hostility.
Omnipotent are we who vanquish time
And space and letterless finality,
With fashioned words for that immortal mime
Where God is trounced in His rascality.
It's true the curtain falls when God inclines:
But first the reasoned rhythm of our lines.

V

Close down, black night, upon these staring eyes
Until the body sinks and, wholly lost,
Shall never feel again the sharp uprise
Of hope that springs into eternal frost;
Here dews of anguish beading bright the brow
Shall never vanish under rising sun;

And welling tears in their spasmodic flow
Can never touch the depth of their own run.
A frozen emptiness now fills the sky:
We have no breath to breathe-in misery;
And if in stifled nakedness we writhe,
We catch the icy whirr of blinding scythe.
Consummate Death, so apt in taking all,
Leave us at least thine own black decent pall.

VI

Is it not time we ceased to label Love,
Trying to fasten sexual counterpart
On each small bud that opens in the soul,
On every cheerful sound that sings above,
On each soft impulse springing from the heart?
What if the fragrance clustering in the bowl
Be but the flowers' fair engendering
Shall this excuse our poor foul maundering?
There is no counterpart of mind but mind;
And Love has surely shed her every lust
Ere she can live and permeate mankind,
Leaving the dead to their fermenting must.
Once I had a friend whom I loved dearly.
Woman or man? O why should I see clearly?

VII

When all men praise thee, then I count it loss;
For how can one add to the voice of all?
But when one blames, then all my gold is dross
Till I have spent it to inscribe thy pall
In golden letters that shall outlive both
Thy fame and myself living, single, loth.
Intemperate my grief; distraught I rage,
Until thy tempered mind inscribes my page;
Then cooled yet sparkling in the clear-eyed morn,
With clear resolve I clearly thee adorn,
My passion moulded to the sinewed line
Of sonnet, or some looser full design:
And if all blame the verse that I indite,
One praises, and this darkness turns to light.

VIII

The beauty that the living eye has missed
Sometime has by some artistry been caught
And thrown an iridescent sunlight-kissed
Remembrance, in all time for all who sought
Beauty, but found it not when beauty passed.
Yet in whatever stuff the artist wrought

To freeze, to catch, to build, he incarnated
In marble, colour, sound or moulded thought
The distillation of a moment, time-translated,
When beauty shone an instant, fixed at last.
The moving corn and bluebells on the hill,
The swallows' turn and evening's yellow fall,
The salty wind's lash and the turning mill,
These I must live: your beauty seen through all.

IX

Imperforate eyes, smooth arching stone conceit,
What can transmute your bleak opacity;
What alchemy can change, what power delete
The marbled film through which you will not see?
Hard staring statues 'mid the entangling green,
We rest our fate upon the springing grass
And, based in blindness on a world unseen,
Look up to heaven to lighten our impasse.
When through this garden set with statuary
Once in an age some quick-eyed man shall stray
What can he find in all this mortuary
Wherewith to work, whereby to pass his day?
Will he not rather rush, a piercing shaft,
Leaving all monuments to wonder why he laughed?

X

Bewildering loss. Again I brush the haze
That films across my mirrored firmament,
Set in the mind to give back as I gaze
Your features in my own clear deep content.
Bewilderment repeats the gesture blind,
Expectant I recall each lineament,
And still your frozen breath films all my mind
Leaving no beauty but your testament.
Impoverished glass, wherein I watch in pain
The hourly thoughts that posture as they pass;
What can enrich thee, what smooth out thy grain,
Rough lustreless congealed reflecting mass?
If only frosty years and frozen duty
Retrace in feathered scrolls at last your beauty!

XI

The shattered remnants of the fallen day
Spread on the sky their darkened citadels,
And twilight hangs suspended over clay
Waiting the faint prick of the star that tells
Of night's succession to diurnal power.
So waits the heart when silence follows on

The cataclysmic fall of some grand tower
Where heart held state in deep protection.
Can that succession hold within the mind?
I care not, if it comes, how late the star
Pricks sharply with the poignance of its kind
This vaulted nothingness, late bright, familiar.
Imprisoned by the ruins, in suspense,
The mind must build again her own defence.

XII

Peace comes so often by a languid stream,
And June makes promise of so deep a store
Of quiet dreams upon these banks which seem
With quietude to bound life's very shore:
Here may the eye, untroubled by the gleam
Of dancing waters, dream and keep no score.
The troubled mind cannot but take offence
Robbed suddenly of June's sweet indulgence.
Inveterate habit of the wayward mind
Now roaming naked, now intent to rest—
Wearied at last of what it cannot find—
Its clothèd thought on clothèd nature's breast.
I never knew the scented winds of June
Could strip so bare her sorrow-laden loon.

XIII

When loveliness informs some mortal frame,
And flesh, an alabaster guarding light,
Transmits this piercing coloured pulsing flame
Through flesh corruptible in flame's despite,
Spirit expands and throws her spoken net
Around this frail flesh-bound translucency,
Where flesh and flame, in time's conjunction met,
Token our uncorrupting fluency.
Distraught by the still vision of your grace
Seen in the heart when darkness fills the eye,
What can control the pulsing maddening race
Of thoughts that interweave now, ceaselessly?
Nought: unless Beauty weaving with her rhyme
Can give her peace on Sonnet's closing chime.

XIV

Enlightening play in radiant countenance
Disturbing all the gloom of toppling years,
What secret springs subscribe their maintenance
To feed that spirit naked among fears?
Steadfast we look into those eyes serene,
Caerulean gates to that imperial hall,

Where mind enthroned once ruled the Damascene,
Or mused observant by the eternal wall.
O radiance, shearing like a damask knife,
Strike on our grief down to the crystal heart
Of flint-engendered truth where vitreous life
Flows comfortless but clean with healing smart.
Then, burning in the caverns of the mind
Let thy truth shine—though chilling all mankind.

XV

And if, primeval through the virgin trees,
We sudden saw the meaning of our fate,
And met it, riding on the morning breeze,
New-born and lusty, naked, without date—
Confirm me, men, on this now yellow page—
Would not our world be turning in a glow
Outshining moon's spleen or this solar rage,
Turning in reason, neither fast nor slow?
And if, coeval with these latter days,
We feel, but do not see, relentless Fate
Steal on our tottering step, that now delays
At some new creed or counterfeit of mate,
Can we be certain in our new despair
That some new sun will not invade our care?

XVI

Endurance is the property of kings,
Whose rule runs straight across these swaying tides
Where other creatures float their tired wings,
Dipping inconstant as each wind subsides.
How seldom in our trafficking with youth
Do we speak one who flies that aureole
Crowning the masthead, carried through the smooth,
Or when the lightning quivers from the pole.
Set in the broken waters of to-day
I caught the glow of this thy diadem,
And made of it my pennant and my stay,
And witness of my one proved theorem:—
"Endurance, only perquisite of kings,
Is greater than the sum of rooted things."

XVII

Desirous only to inscribe your name
For other men who other names caress,
But never knew, but could not praise nor blame
Your many-coloured robe of changelessness,
I will inscribe it in a secret place,
Untrumpeted by common minstrelsy,

I will inscribe it on the living face
Of granite rock that bastions Poesy:
Where, in the fortress that you once loved best
Of all the castles that you made your own,
Shall be inscribed the fortunes of your quest
Whereby all else became a bubble blown?
I choose this facet scored in fourteen lines,
Which man may climb to, but a god designs.

XVIII

And when your fame is surely in the grave,
And all have said the words their heart could spare,
And silence builds her sepulchred enclave
To lock at last what only death could dare,
Irresolute, benumbed, our loves will cry,
Lifting their voice beneath that leaden vault,
Clamouring in leaden echoes wordlessly,
Beating, protesting, with the heart at fault.
Then must the heart find other rags to rend,
Commemorative to flutter at your shrine,
Waiting till silence can at last attend
The consummation where all hearts combine:
And Poetry bestows her parting boon
As, wordless, dark, she still beats on in tune.

XIX

Soft trio playing in my chambered soul!
I cannot rest till I inscribe thy name,
Thine, dear my wife, and thy sweet-toned viol
Whose muted cadence puts my voice to shame.
Our love of him hath unison divine
Lent to the movements of the mounting chord
That strikes across our even day's design
With the remembrance of his vivid sword.
As some slow stream, contained within its shores,
Makes gentle music though unheard of all,
So may our love as gently she explores,
Desolate of his, still murmur musical.
Thus in our sadness may we celebrate,
One lost in one, our sorrow for one fate.

XX

When Mind slips smooth within the coil of Mind
And two minds build their solid traceries,
No longer seems the world a hollow rind
Adorned by fancy's cobweb laceries.
Then stands the substance of twin-plighted dreams
In one imagined fair sobriety;

Then Heaven and Hell hang solid nor do seem
Fantastic weights upon each moiety.
I, who have felt the twisted strength of twine,
Forsake the suppler grace of single thread
Believing nought can ever undermine
This golden filigree in twofold lead.
Unless perhaps that single Alchemist
Erodes in envy what the worms have missed.

XXI

Believing all, believing all your love,
Which never by a word you did declare,
I stand abandoned in that noisome cove
Where sound the seas of terminate despair.
O tawdry credence in what is no more,
Thou seems't a gaudy sacramental plate,
Swung with an incense to bedrug a sore,
Lewd offering of an emptiness inflate.
What piety can chill this hot desire,
Born of a virgin, love without reward,
Not chastened to trim sacerdotal fire,
Burning, an outcast, without bed or board?
Ah true, this flame should sometime flicker out;
But in the grave, but in the soul's first rout.

38

XXII

The quiet mind, lit by the transient ray
Of Beauty, takes no sweet possession;
Contented in its study and her play,
Rejoicing, through the heart's distraction.
O heart, control thy leaping covetous beat,
O mind, enlarge thy wide dominion.
Beauty, O heart, stays not on morning's feet,
And are thy realms, O mind, empyrean?
The heart a torment, and the mind a vise,
Come then, my soul, impassioned in restraint,
This bounding fire and now this binding ice
Resolve, and reunite in one clear plaint:—
Beauty must pass, swift traversing our night,
We weep, but care not—if she follows light.

XXIII

Are you asleep, my dear, in some new bed?
O paltry fancy flickering from the soul!
Are you asleep? Then must I noiseless tread
Around the galleries of this brazen bowl.
And if, a thrall to fancy still, I catch
A murmur through that thick unbrazen door,

You must forgive me if I soft unlatch
A lock that seems to prison all my store.
Forgive you must. Imagination throws
The door wide open on those private seas
Where grief makes traffic, and the biting breeze
Of mind alone controls those icy floes.
For Poetry has come to me again
Imagining she now can calm this pain.

XXIV

And have we found your sum at bitter last?
Finding it frozen in the last redoubt:
Is there a sum to all your figured past
And a congealing as that fire goes out?
Poor memory bustling tends each feeble light,
And miser love counts and recounts her store,
And darkness gains and nought is reckoned right,
The sole addition of our more and more.
Fantastic summing and fantastic care
Relighting candles, when the golden air
Fills all our being as we all draw breath
Deep, deeper, deepest at what men call Death.
Preposterous ghost, how dare you gibber here
When one has smiled and met your own last leer?

XXV

O muttering Time, what—dost thou grumble yet
When nought can stop thy gnawing rhythmic lust?
Thou'st eaten out my heart and eyes and met
The still warm bone to serve as thy last crust.
Fear not, for others surely come to fill
Those jaws. Give me one breath to contemplate
And fashion thee in fancy to my will,
Nearer to life still in these bones innate.
I'd have thee pass, a clear unchanging tune
Whose constant waters roll in brilliant notes
Swift interchanging luminous souls, immune
To grading dimness, as our own sun's motes.
And if thy jaded taste insists on change,
Let it be swift, and not this deep slow mange.

XXVI

Thou dost sustain me, as a hill-side spring
Supplies the small want of the rock gazelle;
And in a dream I hear the sudden wing
Of hill-side bird and scattered grazing bell.
The stinted turf sets in the sunken rock
As, dreaming on, I see the rain-filled cup,

41

Holding those seeds whose little flowers mock
Austerely all the roses where men sup.
Awake me not, O dream by that hill-side,
Endure a little till the evening comes,
And I may lay my wounded thirsty pride,
Night-covered, by that spring where no bee hums:
For flowers are scanty in thy wilderness,
And springs enchant with their own voicelessness.

XXVII

The mirror's cracked, unkempt I'll thrust my way
Right to the hollow of our hallowed truth,
Set on the mount we saw, if clear the day,
Contented as we trudged our pilgrim youth.
Now noon has struck and I must leave behind
Blue outlooks and the tawny springing East,
And see at last if what we saw was blind
Blue piling vapour steaming from some beast.
Shall we find essence from our air distilled
Filling that lair where all our answers lie?
Or will they pounce, but questions, fury filled?
Or will they close, full-lipped, our certainty?
Quick to her heart I now must thrust, unless
Unmirrored, I would grope in sunlessness.

XXVIII

When all the world is metal and I mould
The whole white-hot into one blinding word,
Still from a corner of my workshop cold
A stray wind mocks me, piercing like a sword.
Ah glowing phrases of my mastery,
Still, as serene I count the stars by name,
Some soul untended smokes in misery,
And makes my craft seem but a lonely game.
Now that I weep to melt into one tear
All that you were and ever are to me,
Must I receive into that perfect sphere
One craven doubt to black my artistry?
Never, while the waters roar from melting peaks,
Or heaven at evening dies in molten streaks.

XXIX

Late communing with beauty brightly lit
By the effulgence of a living past,
My dazzled eyes can scarce combine to fit
This present substance and that shadow cast
Imagined by the heart in fullest day,
Upon those hills, in beauty's afternoon.

43

O who can lend these eyes, wide in dismay,
A cover from the fierce night, come too soon?
But if communion with the present dead
Must shake our power of living intercourse,
I know this legion tramping through my head
Shall never leave my soul in bound remorse.
For who can ever, now my bed is made,
Convince and part, his substance and my shade?

XXX

If the containment of the heart exceeds
By subtle magic heart's containing wall,
Some wondrous change then colours all our needs
Transmuting into music's rise and fall
The daily pangs and surfeit of our love.
It matters not, when drenched by this fair spell,
If far from us our loves so lightly rove,
Or beckon some sly secret soft to tell.
It matters not if outrage runs the land
Lasciviously to tear each secret strand
That holds and does not hold two as they stand
Sea-riven or twin-prisoned, past remand.
It matters that your wisdom taught me this:—
Where Love containeth we're content to miss.

44

XXXI

Pretended wrongs must ever solace find
In living back their miserable pretence;
No wrong can blossom in the forward mind
Imbued by spirit, soil without offence.
When wronged by fate we raise our querulous voice
Clamouring for balm no mortal ever had.
How can our wrongs pretend fate had a choice
Or knew, inhuman sot, our human bad?
Now in the garden of this loneliness
May some frail right run shaking all the trees
And touch in human breath on loveliness
And bend the set mind to her reasoned breeze.
Thus even the pretence of sorrow
May be uprooted, freeing our to-morrow.

XXXII

If proud communion of two separate minds
May light by flares the intervening dark;
If darkness drowning all the light she finds
Cannot prevail against the spirit's ark;
If human wisdom, armed to close with fate,
Can of her puissance wrest intelligence;

45

If lovers find, in love without rebate,
Eternity as their just heritance;
May not the mind usurp the judgement-seat
And binding courage on her levelled brow,
Pronounce her verdict, praise or blame, in sweet
Discrimination of this Chaos—now?
And if this treason prove but hell-inspired,
Whose, whose the blame but His, who Chaos fired?

XXXIII

Shall the white palaces of the mind at ease
But crumble to the wind of soul distraught?
And must the heart bear all, some will to please,
That rides in triumph where we men have fought?
Never shall it be said of this dour race,
Now pregnant with a future all unknown,
That, rolled with their original disgrace,
Of ignorance, they yet shall fall alone.
Lashed by the spirit in one whorl of time,
Creator and created feel at last
Falling half human, falling half sublime,
Some common end, on which their shadow's cast.
Conjoined and still on the eternal plain,
Created and creator share one pain.

By loss impoverished, poorer in my gain,
I've spent my love and purchased poesy,
For keeping love I should have proved insane,
And what's the cost of rhyming fantasy?
So all is well, though poet I may yearn
For loveliness unbalanced by account,
Spendthrift of all I'll play, as I can earn,
These flaring words in one gold-minted fount.
For lying spent, close to my emptied ground,
There's all the night to reckon up the cost,
And who knows, buried in that safe's profound,
What I may find of what I've surely lost?
Though this I know—your sum is ne'er the same,
As I recount each poem to your name.

XXXV

Joy shall remain when all the world has gone,
Waiting to murmur with the dying heart
Her gentle cadence, following soft upon
The dying wind, now settling far apart
Beside the sea, that waits no other breath.
Joy shall remain after the tired sun

Sinks in his lustered bed, lit last for Death,
And the rebellious moon reflects no more his run.
Joy may remain though nothing longer reigns,
And darkness holds what light had scarcely won.
Joy speaks at last, though the whole world refrains,
For she hath other powers than one passion.
So in my heart joy settles, homing fast,
When all I love, will love, can love, has passed.

XXXVI

If to sustain an everlasting hope
The soul must reach and breathe another air
Whose confluence soothes but far exceeds the scope
Of mind entangled in this wood too fair;
If Being, subdivided, then must part
Into three fragments ringed by sterile zones,
One breathing air, one by consummate art
Discovering beauty, while the last feeds bones,
Then I for one proclaim that hope is vain
If founded on this jointed trinity.
Truth, seamless, whole, cannot be sold for gain
Or be exchanged for thrice futility.
This you did feel and faced your hopeless end,
Refusing all, this one truth to defend.

48

XXXVII

When specious reason seeks to wean the soul
From brooding on some deep confounding loss,
And weariness waits eager for her dole
Of respite, though she knows that peace be dross,
How oft the soul flies circling, scarcely sane,
Till piety enwreathes her weariness
And makes rough chaos one soft restful plain
Of clouds in all their specious mistiness.
Aid me, stark heroes of the inveterate Grail,
Through body, quit of all, to force my quest,
Staunch when my reason fears the throbbing hail
Of madness, and the spirit seeks her rest.
For body prisoned holds this certainty:
None can play false, if none can find the key.

XXXVIII

A little wind late caught me ill at ease,
And whispered fearsome as I turned the leaves
Of that great book where poets' memories
Are writ to sunder grief from grief that cleaves
And threatens all to blot for one embrace.
The rustling leaves thus whispered as they turned:—

"Beware, in lettering to inscribe his grace,
Lest thou restore the ornament he spurned."
It was a little wind I'll not heed now,
For now that Death himself has stripped thy stem,
O royal poplar of the shivering bough,
What ornament can serve for diadem?
Made puritan by death, I'll yet enroll
All of my art to colour rich thy scroll.

XXXIX

When all the grass is grey, and morning dew
Spreads her untrodden carpet for my feet,
And night, retiring behind curtains new,
Allows fresh traffic in the mind's clean street,
Then might we meet as by some happy chance
Which sets our minds acoursing, each by each,
Carrying us on before the sun's advance
Till, spurring light, we stretch our curving reach.
So might we part while still our splendid day
Holds promise, nay fulfils, in heatless fire
The consummation of two minds at play,
Free of the world and freed of night's desire.
Such was our wish; and now fulfilment's come
The Dawn demands, and I must pay, her sum.

XL

And if at last we've broken through desire,
And freed ourselves of bonds that men can break,
What means this life without its gnawing fire,
What—men, when hearts give nothing we can't take?
And if dawn brings no lust and its begetting
Of noontide heat and twilight's grey remorse,
What brings the night but unredeemed forgetting
Of all we knew while sun could stay his course?
Is there no land in our wide universe
Where this intelligence, once wholly freed
Of hot desire and cold inbreeding curse
Of jealousy, may taste some lucid mead?
O mind released by thine own winds, now lave
This mouth tight cracked as wind-bereft I rave.

XLI

Come Tragedy, roll on your drums of doom!
I'll listen to your fierce long monotone,
And count your beats as one by one they boom
Terrific from beneath your guarded throne.
No ribald beam may dance across your floor,
Suggestive, to that darkening multitude,

Of other realms where the drums' pulsing roar
Evokes no tremors through their solitude.
Ah take me to those realms, great Tragedy,
And be not greedy for a vanquished whole;
Enough that your remorseless melody
Has drowned the outworks of my deafened soul.
Alone within your echoing frowning shade
Spirit lives on, impregnable, afraid.

XLII

Sufficient are the days vouchsafed to man:
He who needs more must be of little worth.
Doth Infancy not ope Herculean
Her eyes, and Youth shake all in busy mirth,
While Middle Years put all to rights again,
Leaving to brief dulled Age, sorrow and pain?
Could mind conceive a better ordering
Of corporal life, this souls' burnt offering?
For through the turmoil, waiting close beside,
Beauty is there to clothe our wrinkled fields
And deck the mountains, like a veiling bride
Mirrored in lakes, while air her colouring wields.
Thus he who thinks life long may look aside;
And all the rest can curse God, justified.

XLIII

Once more if I attempt you as I see
In coloured words for other souls to sense,
This only would I ask futurity,
To spare me pity's foul impertinence.
I need no pity, wrapped within my soul
I carry all the colours of delight,
Wherewith to ornament your chastened bowl
With the enamel of a poet's sight.
If all should praise the colours I bestow,
Intricate flushing bright of face, yet deep,
Compounded of our words fired in the glow
Of a remembrance that is calm as sleep,
It cannot change the quiet quickening gleam
That gilds my memory, deepening as I dream.

XLIV

The searching waters—moved beneath by thought
As tidal she sweeps up each rocky cove,
Or with the ebb embosoming what she sought,
Brings to the sea each separate treasure trove—
Can surely not have missed some jetsom fault
If such did lie upon your granite shore,

53

Yet nothing mingles with the clear cobalt
Of mind at peace imbibing your deep lore.
Restless the waters heave concupiscent,
Icy the wind blows from the mocking North,
Shrilly the sea birds drop reminiscent
Gobbets of sea-dung to befoul my worth.
Out of all soundings rides my poet's bark
Showing, as is required, her one truth stark.

XLV

I've but to turn my eyes when passion brims
And through her teary lenses I win sight.
It is so easy, like to a fish that swims
Straight at the path of some deflected light.
This is no fancy of a waking dream
But living willed Imagination;
In this I live when all the senses seem
Conspiring to impose damnation.
In ecstasy the eye must live by rule
Proportionate to spirit's exultation:
Eye cannot guide but serves, obedient tool,
Passion in torment mastering her frustration.
Thus left sole master of our temporal love
My eyes obedient follow where I move.

54

XLVI

Thou, who didst ever count thyself for nought,
Hast nothing lost in losing all of thee;
While I, who found in thyself all I sought,
Am now made bankrupt by thy loss and me.
Yet, as I starve in penury self-made,
This shall console my thriftless tribulation,
Thou art the same as when I saw thy shade
Pass coolly across my own sun's adoration.
Now is my heart filled with a golden joy,
Remembering all our riches past compute,
A gold content whose gold without alloy
May seem too soft for this hard world's dispute.
It matters not: one heart has left the fray
And the remainder tarries but to play.

XLVII

The robes of dawn now trail before my eyes
The splendour of a fading firmament.
And once again in faint serene surprise
The dawn breeze fans each earthly lineament
Of mountains, lake, and shore I now behold
New-risen apparelling for the Hours' parade,

Passing in classic sequence often told
But seldom seen unsullied by some shade.
This perfect day wherein I hold love's heart
Unclouded by enfolding cerements,
Has dawned, attains her zenith and will part
To leave me housed in night's safe tenements.
There I shall rest and wonder as I dream
From what clear east I'll watch a new sun gleam.

XLVIII

And if I stretch my hand to you in sleep
It is the sequence of the daily wind,
Which now, awakened, moves out on the deep,
Now sighing sleeps upon the wakeful mind.
While there's continuance in earthly things
Who shall exempt this earth-compounded soul
From carrying on her own continuing wings
The privilege and burden of the mole?
So as I touch you with these hands, asleep,
Firm trenchèd in Imagination's soil,
I'd find it strange should I now fail to keep
Tangible, intact, this flower of our own toil:
Perennial blossoming continuity
Of love compounded of our artistry.

XLIX

O living words, where is your substance now,
Which once sustained me as I fought with doom?
Your shadows touch like twilit moths my brow
And leave me hungry in this empty room.
O delicate offspring of the teeming brain,
What nurture can secure your dominance,
In those grey realms of internecine pain,
Which only you can rule with competence?
O proud full-bellied sails, set by our thought,
To carry and preserve what thought has won
From chaos and illusion frenzy-wrought,
Shall wind surcease, nor breathe on that ocean?
Sighing the land wind softly answers me:—
"Death maketh even words seem shadowy."

L

I see no refuge for the soul hard pressed
By following darkness surging from the pit
Where lies the corpse of all that heart confessed
As sole illuminant through Space unlit,
Unless the beauty of the screening day,
Vocal at last, may to the heart expound

The secret kept within her secret sway
Of all she strews in air, 'neath sea, on ground.
Scorn not to shield me, loveliness of words,
For scarce shall I escape the jealous dark
Now lunging towards me with invisible swords
Of demon skill at practise on their mark.
Thee only feeling, seeing, hearing, thee,
May I at least win sleep and sanity.

LI

When trivial pleasures sparkle in our path,
Who knows if they're not drenched with morning dew
Fallen from a heaven whose black habitual wrath
Has stayed for once her clouds of poison brew?
We need no prophet wise in weather lore
To foretell menace to our nakedness,
Nor must experience spend her bitter store
To presage storm from present cloudiness;
But often through a blue rift in the sky
I've seen, and never seen, a brilliant star,
Thinking that nothing but black sorcery
Could show me heaven when night was still so far.
Whereas had I but sunk in Truth's deep well
Down would have gleamed that star without a spell.

LII

The little joys which run about our house
To shelter us through this wild sojourning
May be as small and silent as a mouse
That looks out gleaming from her burrowing.
How often in our busy housewife pride
We sternly stop each private little rent
Whence, but for care, small joys would creep inside
This dreariness wherein our days are pent.
When sweeping sorrow runs through all our clay
And threatens gaping cold destruction,
Let us allow some joy at her small play
To use anew our habitation.
Never shall it be said that monstrous size
Had power to dim a poet's peeping eyes.

LIII

There is no health in us if we endure
Only when cushioned on the multitude,
And what's the certainty we can procure
At cost of soul's rock-bounded solitude?
How many keep in undiscerning pride
The honours possible to herd-creation

59

Presented to the sheep who first have cried:—
"Behold the meadows of our restoration!"
But he whose path leads by the precious grass
Set in the flat rock of the thirsting hills
Has ever left the awed and puzzled mass
Behind him as he thrusts to what he wills.
Can he exchange the uplands of his health
For what the world can give of meadowed wealth?

LIV

O proud prerogative of living pain,
I will not fear to wear thee as a plume:
For living waters bear a crimson stain
When love-a-bleeding flecks the crested spume.
Now as we love swift carried to our end
And hurry past a thousand nodding flowers,
The wind that sways them ruffles as we bend
Our passive breast to pass those darkening bowers.
Deliverance comes with the impartial sea
That lies untroubled to engulf our all,
But till the moment when the life to be
Bosoms our pain, we'll triumph as we fall:
Proud cataracts we'll fling as we suspire,
Plumed waves of realised and lost desire.

LV

But in the stillness of thy love I'll bask
Unravelling all my tortured thought of thee
Knowing that I need only clearly ask,
When clear the answer shall come back to me.
If not in Death where shall a man find rest?
And in thy death I surely lie with thee;
Then quiet must I live to be caressed
By thy still mind and my own poesy.
Which shall outlive the other, who can tell?
I see no shadow yet across my glade,
Where in repose I count thy tolling bell
And listen for the note that's but delayed.
Contemplative, in freedom passionate
I leave thee, as thou wert, exempt by fate.

LVI

In life abstemious, prodigal of self,
For each vice you could show a counterpart,
And for each daintiness of moulded delf
Found some true counterpoise of ruder art.
Bereft of sight I touch this statue set
With jewelled crystals of your artifice,

Whose punctual bite makes lingering hand forget
The absence of a living face to kiss.
You could endure through space where toppling need
Might not o'ersway your balance hour by hour,
But like the clock your life marked deed from deed
With the precision of controllèd power.
The finger points upon your magic scale
From deepest beauty unto beauty pale.

LVII

I have no fame to lay before your tomb
Nor riches to adorn a monument,
Only the children of my spirit's womb
Can make my adoration permanent.
How frail begins each puny prattling line
Designed to bear you to futurity,
Till in my travail line on line divine
Swells to full chorus in my agony.
When peace at last enfolds me in my bed
And sleep adorns the image I adore,
I hold this certainty with all our dead,
That earthly love can never mock me more.
Here line on line lies all I have to give
If it suffice not, we did never live.

LVIII

The short-lived fragrance of the full-blown rose
Can ravish all the peace of passing men
And fill the air with deep full thoughts that pose
Eternal questions of our how and when.
Why must perfection ever clean distil
One bitter burning doubt of permanence;
And all the beauty that our passions will
Suggest the cruel gleam of transience?
Are not our senses testament enough,
When every sense bears its immortal weight,
That we must bargain for the flimsy stuff
Of outworn creeds to clothe our doubting state?
Enough! this catholic rose now scents our night:
Must we protest against some future blight?

LIX

But what may challenge foul adversity?
Is it the hope of better days to come?
Ah me, what has that given but bankruptcy
And adding nought to nought in weary sum?
Can nothing triumph but our whole defeat
Which robs misfortune of her victory,

Or is there in the pit some charm discrete
Which turns to laughter melancholy?
It's certain hope can never break the spell
Of days whose blackness matches but their night.
Hark, in my soul there lives a bubbling well
Which tinkles like an everlasting sprite.
Adversity, I care not when you go
If I may hearken to the spring below.

LX

But if our only enemy is Fate,
O children born into this baleful star,
How then command the legions of our hate
To march upon that fortress twinkling far?
The seas of space fill all the airless moat
O'er which our voice must carry to be heard
In that last parley with the One who smote
The first blow, giving life we deem absurd.
Nay we'll not shout; our breath is scarce enough
For us to gasp out all our hopes and fears.
We'll camp upon the bright edge of our bluff
And daily wash our beauty with our tears:
Till at the last, resplendent with our sun,
We set together with the things we've done.

LXI

Now, lest the mind take charge and vindicate
Her sovereign rights upon this grosser frame,
And send it headlong fused, one mind elate,
Into insanity that knows no shame,
Our being must dip humbly in the mud
Till clothed in drab it can no longer shine
But may endure, a folded fragrant bud,
Breathing a human promise, not divine.
Thus in the long dark days that surely come
Close on the setting of your late seen star,
I'll pay the price due for my mind's ransom,
And lock my heart behind the day's bright bar:
There body snug, and the soul half asleep,
The mind may guard all she may safely keep.

LXII

Where shall we roam? Our happiness is set
With every sail that's carried by those masts
Springing sheer raking from our black hull wet
To carry us together while wind lasts.
"Whither away?" We smile as down the breeze
We catch the hail of all we've loved before

And slowly heeling as we swiftly seize
The freshening gust, I wave towards the shore.
Ah stinging whip of spindrift fantasy,
I am alone upon that phantom ship
And all the gales of maddened Poesy
Can never bring me thy companionship.
Yet still we roam entranced upon this breeze
That blows through time and shakes my memories.

LXIII

But if Time melts into eternity
And deliquescence is the name for death,
How figures fear but as a rarity
Among the sick and those born scant of breath?
What's left of sin when all futurity
Is there, is here, to wash that smudge away
And we must seek another purity
Than the denial of our present clay?
O niggard souls, is your asperity
Sufficient payment for the all you owe?
O dullard minds, your cold banality
But rakes in ashes when this dust's aglow.
If Time's a pimp and Death his one last drab,
Let's live at least as servants of Queen Mab.

LXIV

And who can doubt the omnipotence of thought,
Who ever slept with virgin Poesy
And found in her womb what the world has sought
But none can take save by his ecstasy?
O Poesy now mount your bridal bed
That sways preceding all our caravan
And swing across this desert, beauty led,
Against the hosts of dull, dumb, foundered Pan.
Omnipotent thought that must engender truth,
Your writ still runs through all the sands of time,
And at your wells our whole embalmèd youth
Shall rest and listen to the camels' chime.
And when our journeying begins again
Omnipotence may soothe our present pain.

LXV

I mourn: and cloistered in my raiment dark
I sudden see my quick flesh gleam beneath
Till mourning drops from me, a leaden lark,
And leaves the splendour that you can bequeath.
I must rejoice when all your life for me
Reflected the sane azure of the sky,

Black death insane can never stop my glee
Nor fate enweb me like a wandering fly.
I've but to look at your imagined face
To hear the lark, now high above my head;
I've but to inscribe a line of all your grace
To catch a trilling joy unmeasurèd.
Come then, my sables, wrap me all about:
You never can enshroud the joy without.

LXVI

I need no more the glitter of success
To prove that I am armed against the night;
Need lovers always keep their golden tress
To recollect their loves when out of sight?
I need no proof that substance now can give,
For all my substance has become a shade,
Nor shall I crave for beauty, while I live,
That's more substantial than this love betrayed.
There is no light to show my darkened world,
For all my world is merged into your light;
Nor need I compass, all my sails are furled;
One clear horizon satisfies my sight.
But if I call, then all philosophy
Sinks like a coffin in my raging sea.

LXVII

Beauty is the embodiment of Love,
And spirit mind within that body fair,
And in her functions she may silent move
Content, for speech, to breathe the quiet air.
Why then should Poetry intrude her voice
Upon that perfect, mute, pure functioning
And offer love equality of choice,
Between her peace and golden questioning?
There is no choice, when beauty's heart doth lie
Struck by the poison of a sudden pain:
The heart would stop, and love would surely die,
But for continuance in the beating brain.
Then must all poets speak, to heal and hide
The stricken heart of Love the mortified.

LXVIII

O Moon once more I see your lantern shine
Half-closed asleep upon the Syrian night,
Dreaming within the space you've kept divine
And starless, to enhance your little light.
An eastern velvet clothes the present sky
Pierced sparsely by her stellar glimmering,

And peace enwraps the sleepers as they lie
On terraced stone, by pillars, clustering.
And all night long the river to the East
Flows turbid past her antique citadels
Where basalt rocks present the ancient Beast
Protected by the crumbled brick of Tels.
Here in your youth, asleep by such a moon,
You wove the pattern for your living rune.

LXIX

If from a sleeping god I could snatch power
And run right to the narrow end of space,
I'd there devise a very different flower
From this short life we live to His disgrace.
I'd have no lawns to spread their wide abyss
Far, far beyond the scent of buds which spring
Breaking through earth, determined, shaped to kiss
With comprehending perfume each small thing.
I'd have no wastes to dull the eager eyes,
Intelligent purveyors to the soul,
But every sun should greet with his sunrise
Proportioned flowers to fill the day's cool bowl.
This monstrous unforgivable disease
Of disproportion, blights each small heart's ease.

LXX

No, not the wide sweep of the painter's brush
Can awe us with the scale of its display:
Our dawn full-blooded courses to the flush
Of giants, whose retreat composes day.
Not in the thick lines drawn about our frame
Is found the picture of the soul's despair,
Nor can death's silhouetted patterns maim
The competence of mind, in death aware.
However wide the circling light now wheels,
Steeping full brush into her myriad hues,
The mind, undazzled, asks for night that heals
And does not shatter what the light imbues.
If to another age Thou dost grant this,
We'll die contented in another's bliss.

LXXI

Meanwhile we've but this trivial smudge of flesh
Controllable at times by wavering will,
Wherewith to win through the entangling mesh
Of life incorporate with this granite mill.
How can our substance keep her grain of steel,
This blunt integrity, beneath the stone

Which grinds in time to the eternal wheel
And turns concentric to itself alone?
How could you form of your immortal soul
That burnished flesh endued to bear you past
Blake's dark Satanic Mills where, living coal,
Men ever burn, close pressed and smoking fast?
If one escapes, he is the pioneer
Of a tumultuous host who've banished fear.

LXXII

Love, what is this? O will you never learn
That one perfection must have duplicate?
Of your experience must you always spurn
Perfected self, because of self's true mate?
How can your cloudless eye, unveiling all,
Miss the twin beauty of your double sight?
Are you indeed but the inveterate thrall
Of dazed reflection from your mirrored might?
Here let me prove to all the loves there be,
Though we were perfected in binding bliss,
He still has found his duplicate in me,
And what I've lost in death I'll never miss.
Thus may the mind play master to the heart
And teach perfection of the whole and part.

LXXIII

Yet none shall know the metal of thy mind,
Though through the runnel of a thousand lines
I pour my soul till I have foundered blind
With all the glowing metal of my mines.
'Tis not enough to see thee from afar
However clear a glass may focus thee.
As well consider that we know a star
From erudite earth-borne Astronomy.
If I could make all beauty seem thine own
Still would I lack in this cosmogony
The radiance bred beneath the arching bone
Proclaiming all as one homogeny.
Still must my fire burn on till all is spent
That men at least may know the way he went.

LXXIV

There is no shade in all this sun-blanched land
Wherein another shade may rest and doubt,
For we know all that eye can see or hand
Can feel and touch, and knowing think about.
The stern monotony beneath this sun
Cannot be broken by that sterile moon,

And all our days ring with the things we've done
And midnight brings no respite from our noon.
A shade by day, a shade from night we crave
Wherein self-coloured we may dream our truth,
Proportioned to the pool wherein we lave
The unstained limbs of our love-stainèd youth.
This shade you had in life: there friends could find
Rest, and the coloured fall of tranquil mind.

LXXV

If Poetry is function of our souls
Why must we ask that other men should heed
Those messages whose lightning joins the poles,
Those glittering words that splash from quivering reed?
It is in tempest that we others seek
When all our heaven breaks about our head;
For Poetry lives silent, proud or meek,
Bearing with self till some dear self be dead.
Then must she die unless her voice reach forth
Enveloping the whole content of man,
And measured words ring out to toll the worth
Of passing Love become caerulean.
Then may the sky resume her azure stain
And poetry fall silent like spring rain.

LXXVI

I saw thee not to-day, nor shall to-morrow.
Remembered yesterdays hold but a store
Of sterile gold, prolific if I borrow
Grief to adorn a black and emptied core.
Can any day of all that time shall give me
Contain one coin of all our currency
Struck in the mint we owned before I lost thee,
To compensate this black delinquency?
Passionate conceit of loneliness' dominion
Whereby, a beggar in the days to come,
I ask before I spend my own oblivion
One separate token of our jointure's sum.
Impassioned I demand, nor fear deceit:
Imagination hath no counterfeit.

LXXVII

Must we then part without one healing word
To drop upon this aching wilderness?
I hear no sound, unless of chanting bird
That speaks but music proving my madness.
O muse, bequeathed unto our soaring mind
By all the poets that have lived and lost,

75

I ask of you a boon of different kind
Than you could grant my compeers, passion-tossed;
I do not long to kiss the captive face
Of some dear love who prisoned me a while,
Nor need I gift of eloquence to grace
A graven beauty that did breathe and smile.
Serene in love, now love is gone, I crave
Serenity of words, my tomb to pave.

LXXVIII

Had I your art, never should words combine
To make the pattern of my living thought.
'Tis not in poems that I should refine
The golden metal where my soul had wrought.
However high the wings of rhythm might raise
Some being lightened by an ecstasy,
Your mind saw clearly through the hottest rays
The heavy silting ash of Poetry.
You must forgive me if this grosser self,
Despairing to transmute the living whole,
Now votive lays upon this narrow shelf
The partial emblem of a chastened soul.
Consummate artist, your whole life was one
Remorseless poem burning to the sun.

LXXIX

If I caress an image of the mind
With velvet words and silken euphony,
Do I then prove that I am merely blind
To living beauty's pure diaphany?
If I profess in words that seem sublime
My love for one who died—O long ago,
Must I confess to guilty lust of rhyme
Because these words leave all my mind aglow?
Shall we presume to differentiate
Imagination from life's inmost core,
Unless we first can transubstantiate
Life into death and leave no gaping sore?
When I caress an image, who can tell
Though it be dead it does not live—as well?

LXXX

I see you smile and shake a mocking head
At all the tumult of this beating mind.
Nay do not mock: 'tis not the final dread
That makes me beat upon a God that's blind.
Though I've no faith to see in each sunrise
Ought but renewal of a day-long spite,

My passion grants unto these faithless eyes
The vision of an end that is not trite.
Though dark envelop all our earthly course
Lit fitfully by faith which must recede,
I plunge unblinded by a sin's remorse
Into the abyss unbroken by a creed;
And if faith greets me laughing at her door
She can forgive, no doubt, one sinner more.

LXXXI

But God is blind. Oh stay with me a while
For solemnly I lay upon my soul
This weighty charge that now but makes you smile,
Determined if but once, to pay full toll.
However sharp the claw of Nature strike
And rend anew what she but now has given,
Catastrophe doth fall from like on like,
And all's contained beneath an equal heaven;
But we, whose mind, surpassing every star,
Still reaches out for one embracing Space,
Require of God appearing at our bar
The unifying answer of His grace.
If the All-seeing cannot see this need
All must proclaim that He is blind indeed.

LXXXII

Transparency of liquid swirling glass,
Immobile, yet swift coursing through my veins—
This is your image, and the bending grass
Bows as you sigh upon my inland plains,
Lying so still in afternoon content
Receptive to the shadow of your cloud
Now passing through this placid tenement
Where I refashion you, calling aloud:—
"O fragile glass, whose one upspringing stem
Bore all that content of pellucid thought,
Nothing can shatter my cut diadem
Etched on the surface of the glass I've wrought!"
Liquid transparent mobile fantasy,
Death shapes thee crystal from my ecstasy.

LXXXIII

Nay tenderly, and in soft human wise,
We may recall our gay sure hours of ease,
Now you have passed beyond my present skies
And I continue in these memories.
Should sentiment reach out her clammy hand
To blur with moisture this clear agony

I've but to look upon our common land
And see the dry, stout, rock-anemone.
Beneath this burning sun I have no fears
Wide though I spread the waters of my grief;
They'll form no dangerous pool of slimy tears
To breed the pestilence of blind relief.
Dry are my eyes, sun blasted: yet the night
Big with moist stars, shall quick restore my sight.

LXXXIV

Intoxicant this blood flows ceaselessly
Till spirit's walls become a beaten red,
Translucent and admitting carelessly
Whatever breathes and is not wholly dead.
How shall the petals of this open flower
Hope to imprison with the beating heart
Light whose reflection never stays her power,
Love that from ambient air can never part?
O fairest flowers that this Earth can grow,
Why close your hearts in hot despondency?
See now the air shakes out your crimson row
And sun vouchsafes her cloud-cooled clemency.
Lift up your heads, intoxicated flowers,
Till all your cups are bright with summer showers.

LXXXV

And if the night must close and seal our heart
To light and air and all humanity,
If stabbing joys and slowly healing smarts
Are the whole sum of this insanity,
How can the spirit deign to travel here
From soul to soul to pour her liquid truth
Into our hearts, and hearts we hold most dear,
Visiting impartial both our age and youth?
I did not ask her when this heart was full,
For who surfilled can think on empty night?
And now in emptiness I'll keep my rule
And turn expectant toward your hidden light.
Whether you shine, or be for ever dark,
My spirit turns to yours without remark.

LXXXVI

Yet comfort me, for I have long to live,
And be not angry if I seem to spurn
The daily joys that sweet companions give:
You must be patient if I slowly learn.
I had no need of anyone to teach
When rapture held my willing mind in play

And mocking loosed me, staying yet in reach
Of mind entranced and free of all her day.
So comfort me that I may surely find
Once more the clear dawn from behind the hill,
And animate with joy of fellow kind,
Travel till evening all her valleys fill.
But comfort me, the day with you I'd spend
For dawns and evenings with the darkness blend.

LXXXVII

I covet not the praise of all mankind,
Not though the meadows echo with my song
And youths and maidens dutifully bind
Their newer meanings on my ancient wrong.
I covet not the fame of him who sings
More tunefully from our celestial score,
Nor do I wish for soft white lyric wings
To fleck the blue of heaven where I soar.
Unto your mind discovering all my soul,
I am content to let the verdict lie
With future ages who may see the whole
Which now I lay before you as I sigh.
I covet nought: how else could I have seen
The substance of this friendship that has been.

LXXXVIII

We meet: or else my soul proves but a bankrupt pimp
Who to a whoreless brothel leads his prey.
I'll live: yea, live on though the taut prove limp,
But in the certain hope that alleys grey
Open at last upon some blue-domed sward.
We'll meet, my love, however recondite
May be the place the future shall award
For two to sample their one brief delight.
And if men say that I am but a fool,
Crackling my thorns beneath an empty pot,
Mine to reply that hope must be a mule
And not the ass that crops his thorny lot.
But if my soul betray me at the last
I care not if the future match the past.

LXXXIX

O Peace, come soon but on a wind that stirs
Each leaf composing this thick wall of night;
For mind would catch, though heart, content, demurs,
Each separate rustling screen that blacks the light.
For magic of this wood's confusion
May yet reveal, relenting at the last,

The secret of the spirit's deep intrusion
Before the seal of peace proclaim all fast.
Therefore, sweet Peace, though heart accept thy gift,
The swooning mind still fain would ask this boon:
That at thy coming every tree may lift
A leafy passage for a shadeless moon.
Then mind at last may close her silver eyes
Reflecting intricate leaf-patterned skies.

XC

If fading light may languishing enfold
The dying sky in wreaths of saffron cloud
And leave the world enraptured by the cold
And starry frostiness in velvet shroud,
Why should we fear when light shall fall at last
Aslant the heavy curtains of our bed,
Assured that with the daylight ebbing fast
Flows certitude of night upon our head?
Ah, little fears that tease our afternoon,
Devouring gnats that will not let us sleep,
You were not there at morn, or under noon,
Nor will be as our head falls on the deep.
Enraptured to the last we'll let our eyes
Brim to the certain pallor of the skies.

XCI

Life's own abundance, scattering her all,
Makes us the beggars of our circumstance;
For who knows when she'll break us for a fall
And when command us to appear and dance?
How many maidens wept when Helen died?
And who kept silence after Shakespeare sang?
Our roaring juggernaut has long replied
To those dark questions asked when Christ did hang.
If with my arms the whole world I embrace
Still is my life but one short human span;
And though since youth I've looked in every face
There are but few that I can surely scan.
In life's abundance this makes our despair:—
The very fairest weigh as much as air.

XCII

Then let us care that nothing shall o'ertip
The precious balance of these floating wings
That carry all our freight as safe we slip
Through airy narrows where the Siren sings.
If I should strike my deep love's true profound
I may not linger on that leaden bed,

And if I soar to space bereft of sound
Reason must be my counterweight instead;
Like you who kept safe in your soul prepared
A golden counterpoise for dipping scale,
This reeling merchant world has never shared,
An exquisite precision, not for sale.
And if chance once endowed me with that sight,
Must I fall spinning, severed, in mid flight?

XCIII

A thousand hours could I have spent with thee
Had not our hearts held all, and all to spare,
For Love then seemed to hold the mastery
Of time, in space, through circumambient air.
Slaves are beholden when life flings a crust
And waits contemptuous as they knead a paste
Of their lascivious spittle's slimy lust
Lest ought, that nought, that not a crumb be waste.
Ah me, I'd gladly enter serfdom now
Could I regain the precious liberty
To be enslaved within the throbbing glow
That to ourselves alone owes fealty.
A thousand hours had passed, and yet again
I'd feel, as now, their steady branding pain.

86

XCIV

"Peace, Peace alike unto the slave and free"
Proclaims the azure dome, serenely cast
Over a shadeless earth unstained by tree
On which the final shadow comes so fast.
Blue-prisoned, earth-enchained, we may not see
To the horizon of our pilgrimage,
Certain of this, though prisoners we be,
The Earth is moving to her heritage.
Sometimes the soul may cast into a line
Time's meaning traversing the blank of space;
And mind through ages has but to refine
The eternal metal of those words of grace.
Time to all questioning with peace replies
As she writes softly on our passing skies.

XCV

I am no ocean capable of all
Which at the last may render up my dead,
Carried triumphant on a glassy wall
Thundering shoreward, cresting, ghostly led.
Only an ocean, flattening her foam,
Shall seethe undaunted round the Judgement Seat,

Bearing triumphant, on each glittering comb
Souls of the dead, long nursed in her retreat.
I'm but a river rushing down this vale,
How shall I cradle past these rocks of night
Loves that once mingled, crystalline and pale,
In the hill-waters of my springing might?
Only in Ocean's lazy fertile stream
May every river recollect and dream.

XCVI

The clash and clamour of a brazen wife,
The bugling triumph of successful man,
The victories so frequent in a life
Which never strives but where it surely can,
These hang in brave and storied tapestry
To cover walls which else might show a hole,
And decorate our needy memory
When mind and heart are each divorced from soul.
O may my life not lose this trinity,
The one foundation of our quaking sands.
If I must boast, I'll flaunt this unity
Though all else crumbles in my shaking hands.
Nay I'll not boast; or you will mock at me
Proud of my learning your simplicity.

XCVII

Serene I walk, for you are by my side
—Ah, do not go, for we have all to say.
You are just come upon a flooding tide,
There's all the ebb on which to leave the bay.
I have no heart to tell you all my tale,
'Tis wearisome, I'd rather hear you, sweet;
Though Time nor weariness have power to stale
The mocking smile that marks where I repeat.
Well—I'll begin:—"A thousand thousand nights
Upon a million days have passed, since we—."
I pause to turn and catch your twinkling lights,
And see them guard the bay where we should be.
For night has stolen on my step serene:
And who can tell where we have walked unseen?

XCVIII

If heroes must enclose their quivering flesh
In private armour forged against their will;
If genius tangled in her lightning mesh
   Must shroud the process of her living still;
If honest hearts would leave unlocked the gate
Of their own hearts till liars wander in;

If lovers never seek to stem their fate
Till drowned they choke in cataracts of sin;
Must caution be our one eternal star
Through the dark tempest of our earthly drift,
And craft companion us till, past the bar,
One bold horizon shall at last uplift?
'T will be too late to boast of courage then
When certainty makes courage craft again.

XCIX

Dawn now rebukes me rising up from night,
And lays across my face her scented whip;
With silken lash she lightly stirs my sight
And with those fingers flutters on my lip.
When all the Earth is flushing, feminine,
And I can trace the contour of a hill
Whose bosom baring shows a dewy line
Where morning's lips may lightly touch their fill,
Why do I wallow in this bedless love,
Denuded of all softness and reward,
Save what I take from drifting clouds above,
Save what I keep within my steely guard?
The Dawn replies: unsheathing swift her flame
She smites her slug-a-beds with laughing shame.

C

Once when we twined about the day's new stem
The magic spirals of our different thread,
I felt assured that then I touched the hem
Of all the joys our careless hours would shed.
How could I know that when we spoke our last
'T was not the prelude of the autumn wind
That should have carried us, leaves twirling fast,
Or leaves slow drifting out for snow to find.
And had I known, was there ought left to add
To what lay spread beneath our common sun?
I must be sorrowful, I may be mad,
But who knows better that our all was done?
O fluttering maypole centring our joy,
How can I curse thee when thou wert our toy?

CI

These sonnets then must be our passing bell,
Though I shall ring the changes of this life,
Determined through these poems' turbid swell
To steer my heart to stillness out of strife.
I can but dream, when rocking in the foam,
Of some blue harbour where we'll furl our sails;

I can but look for as I chartless roam
Some anchorage where poetry prevails.
I do not ask that all my days should fade
In long remembering what we might have done,
Content if I can build one perfect shade
To testify against this burning sun.
Then housed at last I'll listen for the chime
Of my one perfected cool closing rhyme.

CII

Men often ask of poets how to find
The loveliness inhabiting the room
Of some entranced and solitary mind
That weaves in pattern on her private loom:
And if by chance the answer is delayed
They laugh in loud and valiant guffaws,
Swearing that poets are but men afraid
To work in metal that must set in flaws.
Straight then let's answer this dear scoffing crowd
Whose stuff's the staple of our woven dreams,
And throwing wide our windows, sing aloud
Till all re-echo in their ordered teams.
Then, as all leave in satisfied debate
We may weave swiftly on, inviolate.

CIII

But still we're bound to answer that great host
Whose shoulders bear the brazen weight of day,
Whose feet are valiant as they range the coast
Rock-bound against the Ocean's flow and fray.
There is no health in us or in our room,
If we inhabit our own solitude,
When cataracting white-ribbed rocks' mad boom
Shatters the air where breathes our multitude.
What soul can listen to our poets' tale,
However drenched with our immortal dew,
Unless we foray first against the hail
That drowns the sky and sets the sun askew?
Then in the stillness following the rain
Our words may fall and knit the soul again.

CIV

The sky seems solid where the thunder cloud
Thickens the blue in pinnacles of air,
And as I look the wind cries out aloud
Bidding me banish all my flimsy care.
The earth is solid where the hills uplift
Their weight against the pattern of the sky;

Nor is there hesitance where shadows shift
Their breadth across those peaks of ivory.
Then what do we, when glory fills our eyes,
To doubt of an eternity of man
Whose soul makes images of airy skies,
Whose certainties may this creation span?
Thus in the west the storm clouds comfort me
Though that pale eastern moon recalleth thee.

CV

The moulded roughness of these stony hills
Lies flushing rose before the slant-eyed sun,
And each harsh valley with blue shadow fills
Till rose and blue meet as their colours run.
A paler green may wash the upper field
And seat the moon still faint from her uprise,
Content to wait until the sun shall yield,
And leave her darkness to bewitch our eyes.
O closing day, thy barrenness is past,
So cruelly betrayed beneath the glare;
These fertile jewelled colours falling fast
Shall recompense thy noon of parched despair;
And evening brings unto my day's lament
This treasure when I feared that all was spent.

Poor traitor flesh, how can you not betray
The spirit striving to burst through those bonds,
Fashioned on some primeval simple day
For men contented to unfurl like fronds
In the green limits of their paradise.
O lovely leaves on the tough stem of flesh,
So perfect in your supple strong device
Of green expansion in a yielding mesh,
Your day is past; no longer may the sun
Through veiling rains descend upon your birth
And gently draw you as the summers run
To the sane discipline of winters' dearth.
Poor cracking flesh, you only can revolt
Beneath this flaming spirit's thunderbolt.

CVII

Shall beauty then forsake our riven frame?
Must loveliness fly from the face of men,
And tortured body sink into the shame
Of anecdotage for some shameless pen?
Shall the proud contour of the veinèd breast
Be but the relic of some past obscene,

And rippling muscles now provide a jest
In catalogues of what once may have been?
Must we regard the limpid mobile eye
As the one instrument that science keeps
Of all that wondrous tender panoply
Wherewith our soul once plumbed the outer deeps?
These questions hang suspended with our fate;
And we must answer, choosing love or hate.

CVIII

Clear through the radiance of a carnal grace
His body answered to my stricken soul,
Though memory must now reveal that face
Since death has served me as God serves the mole.
Clean flashing from that bone-encasèd mind
Through the blue portals of those jewelled gates
I hear, I feel, I see and I shall find
The certain answer that once sealed our fates.
Love that is born of man to man returns
Through every channel of his running blood:
Love cannot leave a naked drought that burns
But girdles all creation with her flood.
And bodies buried steeping under mould
Divide and dissipate return enfold.

96

CIX

My sorrow is a smooth and perfect thing
Carved of the silence that must now endure;
No monument, but a bewildering
Perfection offered to a god obscure.
For sorrow stands when all the rest have gone,
A breathing statue in the halls of doom,
A pale illuminant where radiance shone,
The sole companion of my prisoned gloom.
I would not change a line of all her art
As she accompanies my living breath,
And with those perfect lips that close and part
Dumbly replies to each new thrust of death.
O Sibyl, seated by our springs of fate,
Thy perfect answers leave us passionate.

CX

You have bequeathed a lightning streak of blue
To rob the sky of its assurèd brass,
And left to doubt as measure of the true,
A golden spear-shaft quivering in the mass.
You have forgot in this and this gay heart
Some ribald sharp divine impertinence;

But who may boast the quiet of your art
That lived upon the moment's maintenance?
And now the world remains your clamorous heir
Commanding fate to publish all the will,
And write it out in letters bold and fair
That human wisdom there may read her fill.
In vain: your proud bequests fall not to ease,
But take their heavy cargoes down the breeze.

CXI

Nay here I'll rest and watch your galleon reach
Across the blue bay by my pillowed cloud,
And duly note the quiver of the leach
And quiet wrinkle of your sail, endowed
By all the winds of Aeolus to speed
And drive a furrow through the waste of night,
Coursing unruffled by our shallow need,
Resplendent till you fade upon my sight.
Once more the bay is empty as I dream
And I would rest upon the further shore
While other galleons follow on the gleam
That broke the calm of this caerulean floor.
Pillowed upon the further cloud I've found
I'll turn and dream upon a lonelier sound.

CXII

And if your laughter echoing on the void
Disturb some solemn future equinox,
And other worlds feel suddenly decoyed
By humour flowing from a soul that mocks,
Perhaps our God may turn at last His eyes
Inured to acquiescing creature man,
And closely question each renewed sunrise,
Once adequate for His great circling plan.
Perhaps He waits our holocaust to flare
Outrivalling that sober punctual sun
To prove that we, His soul, bright laughter dare
Against a mind's precision, long outdone.
O of Thy mercy be not too precise
Nor wait to watch till all fire turn to ice.

CXIII

Then let us swing between these hanging stars
And weave a corbeil to contain delight,
Nor seek too close the symmetry that mars
This full procession between night and night.
Free through the air I feel our bodies move
And contemplate each waving fiery line

Until the next obliterate the groove
Traced to the splendour of our swift design.
Thus may our joy fly fondly out through space,
Unshackled from the weight of the sublime,
Careless of all but carelessness of grace,
Moving in measure to an empty rhyme.
So let us weave frail baskets by the light
Of stars that twinkle on our spirits' might.

CXIV

Come, golden words, make music of my pain
That I may swoon upon the tide of sound
Till out at sea I hear the healing rain
Mingle her soft notes with my tears' profound.
There let me rest and listen to the fall
Of silken waters curtaining my grief,
Closing my vision gone beyond recall
To the grey lands of shadowy belief.
Here will I stay and jettison my gold
So I may float and breathe upon the swell,
Sole relic of the storm that did enfold
And threaten all my drowning mind to quell.
O golden words, slow sinking one by one,
Return unto your sea: your work is done.

CXV

There is a longing that shall outlast flame,
There is a sorrow deeper than desire.
I call my dead by a forgotten name
And watch the kindling of a sunken fire.
I see his face against my setting life,
Dark sculptured substance of humanity;
And faith becomes a living glorious wife
To have and hold and mock calamity.
And as the sun sinks lower, and the pale
Cold bitter sky of steel derides our woe,
I'll fashion from the night's star-linkèd mail
A new protection and a fiercer glow.
There is a longing that must outlive power,
Deep rooted like the frail perennial flower.

CXVI

The Spirit droops, and all the World grows cold
While every demon lights his separate fire,
Assured at last that he can now remould
Each particle of life to his desire.
And for a time the busy anvils ring
With brilliant clamour of each world begun

And Satan smiles and spreads an iron wing
To shield his children from the common sun.
The Spirit stirs, upon a restless dream;
And each bright world becomes a paling star
Distinguished only by an idiot gleam
As fear falls swift on each particular.
The Spirit moves; and each distracted thing
Becomes again our sweet continuing.

CXVII

You'd have me write though waters fill each cloud
To break in inky deluge on our head,
And all our air becomes an airless shroud
As poor Creation covers up her dead.
You'd have me write though God Himself prepared
To sear my eyes with His last sinking sun
And night fell final on a black Earth bared
To roll in silence in a race outrun.
Then must I write transposing all my woe,
In present loneliness of blazing noon,
Into one crowded magic midnight show
Presided by the fulness of your moon.
Perhaps the lustre of this lunar scene
May limn in earth a shadow that has been.

CXVIII

O grey rock peak against this autumn's blue,
Uphold the gross solidity of man,
Projecting into space as we pursue
Fulfilment and continuance of our span.
Incising into airiness by weight
I watch your steadfast ageing stalwart earth,
And lay my thought beside you as I mate
My mind to your incisive lonely dearth.
Then as my being steeps in formless air
And leaves the sharp edge of your stubborn might
I'll feel that formlessness is somehow fair
And presently will shape upon my sight.
O barren outposts of the immortal mind,
Can you uphold me as I reach to find?

CXIX

Make music now: for who can hear so well
The soft reverberations of the tune
As we, alone: and there is none to tell
Who'll follow now; or whether late or soon.
Strike out thy note, and through my muffled drums
Shall sound the answer from mortality,

Till all shall echo as the silence comes,
The blended chords of our late sanity.
Though while we lived perfection seemed to gild
Our alternating proud antiphony,
Thy death bereaving gave me strength to build
This tower of sound to quell an agony.
Now as my mourning chimes across the plain
Hearken, O men, and go your ways again.

FINALE

νῆα μὲν ἄρ πάμπρωτον ἐρύσσαμεν εἰς ἅλα δῖαν,
ἐν δ' ἱστὸν τιθέμεσθα καὶ ἱστία νηὶ μελαίνῃ...

"Promptly we launched her into the divine sea, stepped
   the mast, made sail and went...."

ODYSSEY, XI, 2, 3.

FINALE

Of what avail, if to the range of man
We add a thousand million years of light?
Of what avail, if in this monstrous span
Our bodies flower passionate and whole?
Now, in this new-born moment of delight
When youthful suns still strut upon the morn,
Tossing aside the flimsy cloak of night,
Now, as I feel the thrusting bud of dawn
And hold the certainty of perfect bloom,
It nought avails, if swirling from the dark
And still imprisoned fount of years unborn
I now can feel the closing pulse of Time:
For pressing backward from the last of man
The tide of doom must filter through our pores
Converting satin sheen to dropsical
Dull pitting mass of one entangled fear
Of doom to come.

If doom there be no present joy can mask
The secret tremor of the soul at bay;
Therefore uneasily we rise and fall
Upon the surface of our shallow cares,

Afraid to probe, afraid to sink ourselves,
Lest suddenly we stumble on our fate
And know for ever our eternity.

Smiling but still, unyielding to the touch
Of timid hands, but pitying the brave,
The Verities stand near.
O wretched Man, what if the story of five thou-
    sand years
Can show no certainty on the recorded mind,
And the still places of the soul can find
No sure geographer?
Control thyself,
And let the mind swing out to the extreme
Of loneliness, but there contrive escape
From lust of lateral ranging thought cut loose
From tether of the flesh that holds the soul
Enmeshed in body. Loyal to thy fate,
Thus in the days to come thy truth shall grow
Organic, steadfast like the Tree of Life,
Not grasped, not clutched at by the frenzied will
Or wound delirious round an ecstasy;
But fronded yearly by the mind's young thrust
Supported by our pillared satined frame
Rooted by gossamer tendrils 'neath the dust
In moisture of the earth that knows no shame.

Therefore I say until this trinity
Of body, mind and soul shall be achieved
And every fool born of our common stock
Feels his toes tingle while his mind moons on,
Not one shall prophesy the doom of Man.
Therefore O mind that hourly spreads your net
Across the sky in exquisite design,
At each proud knot tied by your firm conceit
Pronounce not on the blue air caught between.
Therefore, O soul that quivers in the night
Forsaken by that airy tracery,
Though you can feel, in truth, that something dark
Awaits that unstained bloodless lacery,
Pronounce not on this white from out your dark.
Therefore O flesh that fills the mind and soul
With noise of anguish, rending as you're rent,
Pronounce not as you work upon your loom:
You have no need to tell of certain doom.

But what shall overtake us at the last?
Shall soul resolve her tremor in a glow,
And mind triumphant blaze her certitudes,
Springing from flesh that holds no anguish now
But the last fear of awful solitudes?
Or shall God, merciful, once more decree
Chaos again to veil His golden face,

While we, transmuted to another race,
May cease, content?

At peace with Time the sight at first distils
A crystal clearness from this frozen world
As glittering entities submit their claim
To the divine inspection of our eyes;
At peace with Time we watch the shape of Death
As a black rock spread slowly on the snow
Her blue shade-patterns as we closer come
And curiously attain her reach at last.

Is all perfection then where Time is not?
O foolish man, for then the terror falls
And nakedness craves for her former cloak
To dim the glory of the unwinking spheres.
How terrible is beauty that expands
Without one flaw the confines of the soul
Whose ever-widening reach engulfs at last
The outposts of our careful sanity:
Until, as image after image breaks
In full effulgence perfectly composed,
We can but feel the throbbing of our growth
And look in vain for some small fixèd wrong,
And seize on death and sanctify her claims
Casting an image of our molten fears

To set up on the silence of the plain.
O figment of the brain, memorial
And witness to the yielding of the soul,
I see you black against the frozen sky
Centring the plain.
Behold the punctual multitudes proceed
Worshipful, self-doomed, to lay at your rock base
Lives that would else have been co-terminous
With all.

O Reason which shall save us at the last,
Fair reason, architect of all our past,
How can you falter within reach of all
And stumble back, blind cretin, on a faith?
However far the forgèd links may stretch
Somewhere the light must weaken into dark
And tired vision make an end of thought.
Is weariness a just excuse for faith,
Dethroning reason for her spawning brood
Of facile fancy twisting like the eel,
Bereft of all but their tenacity,
Which broken once, is dead, is limp, obscene?
Nay let us rather trace with tingling pulp
Of living fingers each clean tested link
Unto the end where reason's self demands
Respect for the proportioned loyal mind,

Self limited, percipient of the flesh,
Soft vehicle of adamantine will,
Which else must fall deep through the universe
And hurtle incoherent on the void.

But if we speak her softly ere we part
And ask of her a talisman through space,
Sighing our gratitude for all she wrought
And softly touching her still twilit face,
She will entreat Creation once again
To leave with us this measure of her grace
Whereby, as the last link drops from our hands
Our reason turned to spirit understands
And walks abroad in countries mapped anew.
It cannot be that all the golden rules
Of exquisite proportion and delight
Shall break like brittle steel beyond our sight
Convicting all—and God—of being fools.

We triumph in the pulses of our blood,
We triumph in the riot of our thought,
The thrust and passion of our tempered limbs
Bear us in triumph through each ceding nought.
The air wraps kindly round our new desires
That throb and poise and settle softly down
On meadows where the fountains play in fire
Spouting serene in measured ecstasy.

So runs our life; and reason set between
Exalts her structure motionless, sublime,
With all her coralled royal galleries,
Whose every chamber holds in sweet content
The sea proportionate to severed space
Enclosed by the fine scission of the mind.
Therefore commensurate with running life
Must reason build her tissued citadels;
And nought can follow but black hollow death
If she escape the body's deep embrace.

Therefore when all have set up on the plain
This hollowed image, high concupiscent,
It is no idol of a nightmare fear
Prolonged unduly through the human day
But the proud symbol of our sanity.
Sublime convention of imagined death!
How else could we enjoy our mortal years
And build our crumbling tenements of flesh
And watch the light in rainbow through our tears?
Without this death that shakes our minds asleep,
Asleep upon this earth that pillows dreams,
We should not wake but dream infinity.

Housed in this flesh between two walls of glass
We draw the curtains screening happiness

From the wide night and the too burning day.
And when these twain shall duly blast and sink
The darling habitation of our souls,
Reason herself shall wrap us in her flame
And bear us to a new eternity.
No longer then need we see on the plain
That ghoulish image of disordered thought,
Which stands communal in its civic black;
But each may fashion in his private mind
Some trivial artifice to bind delight
Some golden replica to ornament
The unkempt garden of the immortal mind.

O little jewels of our temporal life,
Facets of luminous reflectiveness,
Not for the radiance of eternity
Would I exchange your many-coloured glass.
Time, time enough when time can no more sting
And eat out with her acid slow distilled
The amorphous matrix of each brilliant joy,
To sink in ocean's dim beatitude
And yield to God the smallness that is ours.

It needs no Christ hanging in His despair
To raise us on the curling brim of dawn
And launch us on the hours that heave and pass

And leave us washed in temporal peace that lasts
While dreaming of the all we can assay.
For we may know, unbuoyed by some new faith,
Unpunctured by some future needling thought,
The certainty of life's aboundingness.
We need no priest: the soul's clean glassy jet
Sprung from the centre of our marble brain
Shall touch as it o'erflowers the formless air,
And fall assured, brimming our circled sea.
Surveying entities twin-cut and clean,
Divided from the nutrient formless air
Intelligence can ask no more of God
But her projection through eternity.
Then can the soul take up the drooping thread,
And stretching taut vibrate her single note,
And shake our being, dropping into sleep,
Until we wake and stirring with the breeze
O'erpass again this ruffling teeming life,
Or tired perhaps by knowing too much strife,
Wing lightly skyward through the shivering trees.

O peace now listening for our mind's call,
You are not deaf but true-percipient,
You have no ears for noises that enthrall
The vulgar, blustering, or too sentient
Spirits attuned to minor chords that fray

Poor brittle minds, whose sapless roots display
Strange frenzied patterns on the cool blue sky.
Peace shall attend us, all whose anguished cry
Revolts at the heaped misery of man,
And in their anguished loyalty to clan
Recall the loveliness of all their peers.
Peace now attend our proud tumultuous hearts
That beat in time, in time, to little years.

Frail beauty set within this ring of steel,
I know no counterpart to thy content,
No galaxy of stars can draw these tears
Or vie with fading colours duly spent
That tinge the raiment of our chosen dears.
Not size or weight or the enormous span
Of sempiternal planets in these skies
Can touch the more eternal heart of man
Or fill the small cup of our deep surmise.
My tears on frosty nights are frozen dew,
My glory blazes in the short-lived sun
And wonder upon wonder comes anew
Through the fresh prism of the day begun.

Pale flows the light of immortality,
No rival to this daily burning day;
It flows inhuman like some metal stream

Past every hovel of humanity.
Yet by its glare so steadfast and so cold
The spirit tests the sparkle of each gem,
Kept in the velvet of our prisoned life.
O fearful stream, no wonder flesh would hide
Her frail complexion from thy simple stare,
Whose stern intense monotony would blast
The truest rose this mind can ever grow,
But for the soul's translucent shielding wall.
Remorseless flood! that will not let us rest
By cultured coppice or the silent stream
Of sense, that now reflects the glitter of a dream,
Now vocal, lips o'er some vicissitude;
O that the fitful breathing of our will
Might blow a true wind towards that icy north
And hold us there, free poised, above thy stream.

Distinction, true creator of our world,
Though death be thy penultimate conceit,
I can forgive thee, for thy loveliness.
Whether thou walk abroad between the stars
And threaten reason with their multitudes,
Or dally with us by a neighbour's brook
And make us watch a straw's vicissitudes;
Whether we plunge into our blood's abyss,
And staring eyes count cells of misery,

Or swift transmuted into hollowness
We catch a note and echo symphony,
Thy loveliness is there.

When rain-drops furrow down the window pane
And lightning scrawls upon the distant wall
Thy loveliness doth overpower me,
And I may give no thought to death at all.
For happiness can use distinction
To light the peep-show of her warm lit house,
Shut in for ever from extinction,
And privileged as any schoolrooom mouse.
And yet, and yet, when happiness is gone,
Once more thou sittest on thy glassy throne
And as thy sceptre points, we see again
The clean division of mortality.
Then to our eyes all loveliness turns mad
And folly rattles on our window panes
While science stalks heroic without end.

Therefore, Distinction, giver of our all,
I challenge thee, cold creature of our brain,
Nor shalt thou reign to terrify this mind
Whatever be thy bounties to the crowd.
Distinguish death, or thou art but a clown
And we the dupes of imbecility,
Distinguish death, clean cutting as thy wont

On both sides of this boasted entity,
Dividing death from life, and death from all,
Then give us back our one eternity.

Roll on round world within this ring of death.
You must suffice for this round-bellied man,
Within whose maw distinction now provides
Sufficient matter for his human plan.
But when his spirit feels the bursting bud
Of youth's wild rose that opens to the dew,
Eternal morning shall alone suffice
To hold the orbit of his paradise.

O poet's words, pure spirit's orchestra,
You need no instrumental panoply.
By mind engendered in the womb of sense,
Your issue sounds upon the pensive heart
Note after note with spinet's clarity.
Of steel begotten, you might not endure
Beyond the noisy age of iron man,
But for the flesh ingrained that holds the core
Unbroken against mode's hostility.
On you we lean when mind is forced to fly
Before the fury of those hosts of sound,
Where music would envelop, leave the ground
And carry us beyond the strength we found
In sober practise of our artistry.

To you we come when flooding years withdraw
And leave us in the salty pools of thought;
On you we rise in passionate grim youth
Finding in flesh and steel the blend uncouth
Which may alone embrace our misery.

O fading colours of a painter's dream,
Too zealous mimic of consuming flesh,
What anguished eyes have watched your colours start
And flush and pale, betraying their own art.
The rotting canvas and the flaking wall
Sustain and break, grimacing as they fall;
Though galleries throughout can testify
To full-lipped pleasures of the inward eye,
The scattered attics hide in private dust
The masterpieces of the men who must.
Wet aromatic swirls of flattened paint,
You sweep in flood of one smooth-chromed delight
Or froth particulate on edge of sight
And drown these naked eyes in coloured tears.
Who shall repay your benison of light
Laid smooth, laid million-pointed, on our night?

What is it that calls to me
Out of desire,
Telling me of power to be
Fountains of fire

Spreading out for all to see
Laked crimson ire?
Gently now my meadows run
With little streams
Pouring in the lake as one,
Quenching all dreams,
Leaving me as I've begun
Cracked full of seams.

Is there no other way
To live with Time,
Shall never night and day
Respond and chime,
Learn the smooth interplay
Of this short mime?

Our steps are sure, though one may cut the rock
A lifetime to secure his one degree,
While others glide in never faltering race
Up airy avenues that hold in space
Their bodies self-contained in airy grace
Of swift-foot pedigree.
Each step is sure, though mind herself must fill
And burst the circle she herself has drawn,
Before we set our feet where only will
Can stand in nakedness before the dawn
Of some new day that heaves up on the still

Perfected sky
Some monstrous orb glaring incongruous.
For, as the constellations break and reel
In terror from their newly risen lord,
Our spirit from her small-voiced corner mocks
Grandeur expanding to a size that once
Impressed the folly of a former might.

O lyric love, transcending tragedy,
Speak to my heart of little things again.
In your minute clear gossiping refrain
All may refute this heavy mystery.
O lyric love, your miniatures shall fade
When earthy particles shall feel no more
The round cohesion of a globe that's stayed
On the precision at Creation's core.
Inform me then of each precise delight
That pricks the pattern of your loveliness,
And I will guide thereby my wandering sight
Through the dark temples of our godliness.
Preserve me in the specious dome of gloom
When soulfulness enwraps the crystal soul,
And all day long we quarry for a tomb
Persuaded that at last we see our doom!
No width of vision, depth of hell shall span
This glinting sprawl of matted particles;

No warmth of love, no wealth of love, no man
Shall ever smooth death's separate icicles.
Confounding urge to ring infinity
With pensive circles of the enclosing mind!
Not eyes, but throbbing contiguity
Can hold apart the beauty of mankind.
Despair not of our soul, O lyric light;
Shine from each facet of our roughened sea,
And we will give slow movement to our sight
And trace in sound your brilliant filigree.
Play out the small notes of your infant scale
And from the sun we'll catch each trembling mote
And ride celestial on the comet's tail.

Deprived of you the mist falls soft between
Each tessellated glow that patines life.
Sad monochromes of thought stain the unseen
And mind makes havoc like a blunted knife.
O when we drown and from our ocean bed
Watch each small beauty sink upon our trail
And silt around our smothered charnel head;
O when we feel to find and finding fail
Upon each contour of our lyric thought,
Despair befriends us and we, doubting nought,
Pronounce upon the light beholden air.
We know delight and build upon a dream

We drown, and ask an island of the sea;
Cloud palaces and dungeons submarine
Alone reward this yearning fantasy.
But if we run upon the wet packed sand,
Naked for once of all philosophy,
Each leaping thought shall leave a welling brand
As we run on salt-lashed by ecstasy.
Clear printed, deep-enduring till the tide
Moves his slow state to set another shore,
Our work shall stand, compounded monument
Of wet delight in firm embodiment,
For those who, seeing all, despise the more
That threatens to o'erwhelm in light, in dark
In fire, in ice, in music's cataracts,
The poised desire of contemplative man.

O little beauties of our rounded home
Rolling so smoothly past these jaggèd stars,
O little treasures scattered on this loam,
We fear no rivals that may light the dome
Of our immensity with monstrous phares.
Sufficient is our spirit to attain
The faintest peak of each still spouting range
That guards the central crater of despair.
Sufficient springs our strength from littleness
To stalk unheeding through a giant world

And stake our all upon a plan close furled,
Destined to fly above futurity.
Proportioned man, behold thy heritage.

Once more O idol darkening the plain
We sit content beneath thy clean cut shade,
Safe from the glare of our eternity.
How sweet to rest when we have travelled far,
How sweet to die when we have lost our star,
How just to meet at the black judgement bar
God, or this Chaos' own finality.
And as we talk, our own adventurous mind
Explores the hollow entrail of thy might;
We listen to its echoes unaware,
Stumbling alone through passages of fright,
Until, until we hear a laughter blind
Above the dome, high in a frosty air.
O reckless mind, of what avail to build
This costly monument to thought's decease,
If with that laughter all begins again?
Come let us gather round the ruined base
And calm the fears of weary witless men
Who now have lost their one security.

      Relive your fears O men
      With death away;
      Smile at your loves and then

Take all away
And find them close again
Where they shall stay
Secure, not in a pen
Like sheep that stray.
Resuffer all O saint,
With death away,
Enliven your complaint—
There's all the day—
Revive each sinful taint:
Sin's come to stay.
Heroes, no more alone
Now death's away!
The people surge and moan,
Heroic, past the bone;
No Christ need now atone,
Death melts away.
While spirit pale at bay
Smiles at the maddening drone
That hums O ceaselessly.

O echoing caves of madness where the mind
Reaches with fingers taut and slanting toes
For some opaque tough alien thing to hold,
To touch, some small beginning left behind.
I do not ask that, prematurely bold,

We should outstare the iron face of death,
Far better to desist and let enfold
The shadowed image round our failing breath.
But if the misery of our decline
Shall geld the potency of rising men,
And history must gloomily repeat
The fairy story of the Night's Defeat,
Then let the caves of madness brightly ring
Until the echoes crack the silvering
Of this black image dressed with saints' alloy
Of Christ victorious over earthly joy.
Shake out wild laughter and bring down the dome
Of every late inhabited rock-thought,
And as we waver shadowy astray
Like drowning bodies sinking to decay,
We'll find some small forgotten alien thing
Whereon to found a new dominion.

> Some small forgotten thing—
> No need for death—
> Some hollow, harbouring
> A poison breath,
> That needs refurbishing
> With a caress;
> Sufficient centring
> For worldliness.

I see the splendour of my soul
As a round world of burning fire,
And take no thought of God's desire,
Turning in solitude, one, whole.
No alien dust can film my eyes;
Integral pure beatitude,
Alone without similitude
I watch each new-born thought's uprise
And know for ever that it's true.
What alien might may then prevail
Against this fortress-crucible
Whose fusèd brilliance cannot fail,
Containing the imaginable.
Ah, let it burn its small fierce flame,
Till, overwhelmed by ecstasy,
It leaps perfected from that mould
To plunge anew where thoughts uprise,
O'erweighted with the dross of care,
O'erfilmèd with the dust of years,
O'erleavened with fermenting tears,
Till once again the soul must burst
Out and above the murky earth
And find perfection in the nude.

O subtle interpenetrating soul,
How soon we lose and find and lose thy power

Following the pattern of thine interplay.
Not memory, not faith, not reason now
Can guide our steps slow slipping into dark,
Nor any shape of loveliness can quell
The frightened murmur of the halting heart.
Then as the languid motion of the blood
Prepares to leave each lovely room of sense
And darkness unopposed slow filters in,
Sweet Courage's self may loose her knotted might
And lay aside all faith and every right;
Till, free of care, our passage she'll beguile
With the free gift of her whole gentle smile.

I do not ask of thought to stultify
The chiselled work of all these biting years,
Because, poor flesh-bound thought, there's no
    reply
To the last question of connecting tears.
As each proud aeon writes her latest line
And stares dry-eyed into obscurity,
The truth shall flood deep-welling from the brine
Which joins the islands of each clarity.
Truth pouring upwards shall at last distil
The perfect globe reluctant from the eye,
Forsaking thought, her reason to fulfil,
In the slow spilling of eternity.

O crystal sphere transmuted from this clay,
Contain us as we perish on our day.

Let us fling out firm seated, supple limbed,
Our largesse on Creation's misery,
And it shall fall a deluge rainbow rimmed
To wash the hollow of each mystery.
We have enough to drench the eternal rock
Till every cranny shall unfold her flower,
And gleaming wastes of the unfissured block
Gather their satin folds into a tower.
See, as the runnels swell, the sun himself
Unveils to build his pediments of mist,
And fiery tongues leap up from shelf to shelf
Gilding each liquid instrumentalist.
Thus as we fling our all upon the air
We leave to darkness only what we spare.

O will of man triumphant over all
But the quick shudder of the sudden beat
Of purpose, set to travel past recall
The dim straight path unmarked by human feet,
Be patient as we quiver, nor forsake
The faithful heart that carried us so far,
Now as we turn beside the light-fringed lake
To plunge into the wood without a star.

Perfect thy triumph that the mind may swing
In even beats through all our certainties
Until it rest at last within the ring
Of one gold lake reflecting dark the trees.

O will of man, endure this moment now
As the first shadow comes, and chills, and leaves
    the brow.

For EU product safety concerns, contact us at Calle de José Abascal, 56–1°, 28003 Madrid, Spain or eugpsr@cambridge.org.

www.ingramcontent.com/pod-product-compliance
Ingram Content Group UK Ltd.
Pitfield, Milton Keynes, MK11 3LW, UK
UKHW012334130625
459647UK00009B/283